SANJEEV KAPOOR

# IRON-RICH RECIPES

In association with Alyona Kapoor

Popular Prakashan
www.popularprakashan.com

Published by
POPULAR PRAKASHAN PVT. LTD.
301, Mahalaxmi Chambers
22, Bhulabhai Desai Road
Mumbai - 400 026
for KHANA KHAZANA PUBLICATIONS PVT. LTD.


First Published 2014



(4377)
ISBN: 978-81-7991-818-0

Design: Anjali Sawant
Photography: Bharat Bhirangi, Dilip Yande, Mangesh Parab, Sanjeev Nadkarni, Swapnil Naik and Vikas Shinde

PRINTED IN INDIA
by Sai Print 'O' Pack
New Delhi - 110 020

# AUTHOR'S NOTE

There are certain conditions when a human body needs iron-rich food to meet the nutritional needs. Why is this so? Because it (as part of the protein haemoglobin) carries oxygen from our lungs to the rest of our body. It also helps our muscles to store and use oxygen. Too little haemoglobin in the blood, a condition called anaemia, afflicts a large percentage of Indian women.

There are certain stages in our lives when our body requires more iron. Infants and toddlers need more iron because their growth rate is rapid. Pregnant women have higher iron needs and are advised to take iron supplement. When people lose blood they lose iron too and therefore need to replace it.

Intake of iron through natural ingredients is very essential and so we decided to compile these recipes especially for you. Keeping in mind that breakfast is the most important meal of the day, it is imperative that this meal should be nutritive. So start your day with glass of Banana and Fig Milk Shake and Green Pea and Carrot Dalia if you are a vegetarian. For the non-vegetarians we would suggest NRG Milk Shake and a Grilled Chicken Sandwich. Not only are these recipes rich in iron, they are tasty and quite easy to make.

So start your day right and have a great day ahead.

HAPPY COOKING!

# CONTENTS

## Snacks and Starters



## Main Dishes

# NRG Milk Shake

**Iron Content: 8.5 mg**

**ingredients**

4 cups chilled milk

4 *chickoo*, chopped

8-10 seedless dates, chopped

2 tablespoons sugar

4-5 almonds, blanched, peeled and slivered

**method**

Place the chilled milk, *chickoo*, dates and sugar in a blender jar and blend at full speed till smooth.

Pour into tall glasses, garnish with the almond slivers and serve immediately.

# Banana And Fig Milk Shake



**Iron Content: 8.2 mg**

**ingredients**

3 ripe bananas, peeled and chopped

12 dried figs, soaked and chopped

3½ cups chilled milk

2 tablespoons sugar

2 tablespoons honey

Crushed ice

**method**

Process the bananas, figs and half the milk in a blender.

Add the sugar, honey and the remaining milk and process again.

Add the ice and blend again.

Pour into individual glasses.

Serve immediately.

# 8 Pineapple Coconut Smoothie

**Iron Content: 15.3 mg**

## ingredients

1¾ cups unsweetened pineapple juice

8 tablespoons thick coconut milk

8 tablespoons shredded tender coconut flesh

2 cups vanilla ice cream

8 tablespoons chopped pineapple chunks

16-20 tinned cherries

Crushed ice, as required

## method

Process the pineapple juice, coconut milk, coconut flesh, vanilla ice cream and ice in a blender till smooth.

Pour into individual glasses or tender coconut shells.

Serve, decorated with pineapple chunks and cherries.

# Green Pea And Carrot Dalia



**Iron Content: 13.9 mg**

### ingredients

1 cup broken wheat

½ cup shelled green peas

2 small carrots, diced

1 tablespoon oil

1 teaspoon cumin seeds

1 small onion, chopped

1 medium tomato, seeded and chopped

Salt to taste

2 teaspoons butter

2 tablespoons chopped fresh coriander

### method

Soak the broken wheat in two cups of water for thirty minutes. Drain. Heat the oil in a pressure cooker and add the cumin seeds. As they begin to change colour, add the onion and sauté till the onion turns translucent; add the green peas, carrots and tomato and sauté for one minute.

Add the broken wheat and three cups of water; add salt to taste. Bring the mixture to a boil, fasten the lid of the pressure cooker and cook till the pressure is released twice (two whistles).

When the cooker is cooled completely, open the lid. Stir in the butter and chopped coriander and serve at once.

# Palak Puri With Tamatar Aloo

**Iron Content: 16.8 mg**

**ingredients**

**Puri**

1½ cups whole-wheat flour

15-20 large spinach leaves, blanched and puréed

Salt to taste

1 tablespoon oil + for deep-frying

**Tamatar Aloo**

2 large tomatoes, chopped

4 medium unpeeled potatoes, diced

2 tablespoons oil

1 teaspoon cumin seeds

1 inch ginger, chopped

½ teaspoon turmeric powder

1 teaspoon coriander powder

½ teaspoon cumin powder

1 teaspoon red chilli powder

Salt to taste

**method**

Mix the spinach purée with the flour; add salt and one tablespoon of oil and knead into a moderately firm dough. Cover the dough with a damp cloth and leave to rest for about ten minutes. Divide into sixteen equal balls (*peda*) and roll into four-inch round *puri*.

Heat oil in a non-stick *kadai* and deep-fry the *puri* over medium heat. Drain on absorbent paper and serve hot with *tamatar aloo*.

To make the *tamatar aloo*, heat the oil in a non-stick pan; add the cumin seeds and tomatoes and sauté for a few minutes. Add the ginger and continue to sauté for a while.

Add the potatoes, turmeric powder, coriander powder, cumin powder, chilli powder and salt. Stir to mix and add two and a half cups of water.

Cover and cook over low heat till the potatoes are done. Serve hot.

# Gur Ki Meethi Kadak Puri

**Iron Content: 18.6 mg**

## ingredients

2 cups whole-wheat flour

¾ cup grated jaggery

A pinch of green cardamom powder (optional)

¼ cup pure ghee + for deep-frying

## method

Mix the jaggery with three-fourth cup of water in a non-stick pan and heat the mixture gently over a very low heat till the jaggery melts completely. Strain.

Place the flour in a bowl and add the green cardamom powder.

Rub in one-fourth cup pure ghee till the mixture resembles breadcrumbs.

Add the jaggery mixture and knead into a stiff dough. Cover with a damp cloth and allow the dough to rest for half an hour.

Divide the dough into sixteen equal portions and shape into balls. Roll out each ball into three-inch *puri* and prick on both sides with a fork.

Heat sufficient ghee in a non-stick *kadai* and deep-fry the *puri* in moderately hot ghee till golden and crisp. Drain on absorbent paper.

Serve hot or cold.

# Crunchy Fruit, Yogurt And Cheese



**Iron Content: 18.9 mg**

**ingredients**

2 large apples, cubed

½ medium muskmelon, cubed

2 large bananas, cubed

2 large pears, cubed

3-4 plums, pitted

2 sweet limes, pith removed, sliced

2-3 tablespoons honey

1½ cups thick yogurt

½ cup cream cheese

2 tablespoons strawberry crush

5-6 sweet biscuits, crushed

8-10 prunes

**method**

Combine the fruit and honey in a bowl.

Whisk the thick yogurt in a separate bowl. Add the cream cheese and strawberry crush and mix.

Reserve some crushed biscuits for garnishing and add the rest to the yogurt mixture.

Partially fill a stemmed glass with the mixed fruit; add a few prunes. Top with the yogurt mixture. Arrange another layer of mixed fruit, topped with yogurt mixture.

Garnish with a prune and sprinkle crushed biscuits on top. Serve.

# Chicken Sausage Rolls

**Iron Content: 26.7 mg**

## ingredients

4 hot dog rolls

4 chicken sausages

2 tablespoons oil

1 head lettuce, shredded

2 medium onions, chopped

4 tablespoons tomato ketchup

2 teaspoons English mustard paste

1 jalapeño pepper, chopped

## method

Heat a non-stick *tawa* and a non-stick frying pan. Slit the hot dog rolls without cutting through and toast them lightly on the *tawa*.

Heat the oil in the frying pan; add the sausages and sauté till golden brown on all sides.

Place some lettuce in each hot dog roll.

Place a sausage and top with onions, tomato ketchup, mustard paste and jalapeño pepper. Serve immediately.

# Grilled Chicken Sandwich



**Iron Content: 8.8 mg**

## ingredients

300 grams boneless chicken breasts, sliced thinly

8 slices brown bread

Salt to taste

8-10 garlic cloves, chopped

1½ teaspoons red chilli flakes

1½ teaspoons dried mixed herbs

2 teaspoons olive oil

4 tablespoons mayonnaise

2 tablespoons tomato ketchup

4-5 lettuce leaves, shredded

Butter for grilling

## method

Marinate the chicken with salt, garlic, red chilli flakes and dried mixed herbs. Set aside for ten to fifteen minutes. Heat the oil in a non-stick grill pan. Place the marinated chicken on it and grill till golden brown on both the sides.

Take it off the heat and set aside to cool. Shred the chicken into small pieces. Add the mayonnaise, tomato ketchup and mix well. Add the shredded lettuce and mix well. Divide the mixture into four equal portions.

Place the mixture on four bread slices and cover with the remaining bread slices. Apply butter on top of the prepared sandwiches and grill in the preheated sandwich griller till golden brown and crisp. Cut into triangles and serve.

# Hearty Bites

**Iron Content: 9.6 mg**

## ingredients

2 hard boiled eggs

½ medium onion, finely chopped

5-6 French beans, finely chopped

½ medium carrot, grated

5-6 spinach leaves, blanched and chopped

1 tablespoon cornflour

½ teaspoon salt

½ teaspoon black pepper powder

½ teaspoon mustard paste

2 teaspoons tomato ketchup

1 cup fresh breadcrumbs

Oil for shallow frying

## method

Grate the boiled eggs into a bowl. Add the onion, French beans, carrot, spinach, cornflour, salt, pepper powder, mustard paste and tomato ketchup. Add the breadcrumbs and mix well.

Divide the mixture into eight equal portions and shape each portion into a heart shaped *tikki*.

Heat the oil in a non-stick pan and shallow-fry the *tikki* on medium heat till golden brown on both the sides.

Drain on absorbent paper. Serve hot.

# Breakfast Wrap

**Iron Content: 22.1 mg**

## ingredients

4 tortillas

2 teaspoons olive oil

1 large onion, chopped

1 large green capsicum, seeded and diced

Salt to taste

Black pepper powder to taste

1 cup grated bean curd (tofu)

1 teaspoon Tabasco sauce

1½ tablespoons tomato ketchup

1 tablespoon chopped fresh parsley

½ cup grated cheese

## method

Heat the oil in a non-stick pan and sauté onion and capsicum till soft.

Add salt and black pepper powder to taste and mix well. Add the tofu, Tabasco sauce, tomato ketchup and parsley. Mix and cook over high heat, stirring continuously, until tofu is firm and heated through.

Place one-fourth of the filling in the centre of each tortilla and sprinkle one-fourth of the grated cheese over the filling. Roll the tortilla up and serve immediately.

Chef's Tip: You can use regular *roti* instead of tortillas.

**Note:** As the name suggests it is an excellent food for breakfast providing protein, vitamins C, A and B, iron and calcium. Being multi-nutrient it can be given to growing children, teenagers and pregnant women.

# Scrambled Egg Cup

**Iron Content: 15.9 mg**

## ingredients

4 eggs, beaten

4 small whole-wheat burger buns

2 tablespoons oil

1 inch ginger, chopped

4 garlic cloves, chopped

1 medium onion, chopped

1 large tomato, chopped

1 teaspoon red chilli powder

Salt to taste

2 tablespoons chopped fresh coriander

2 tablespoons melted butter

4 tablespoons white sauce

## method

Preheat oven to $180^0$C/$350^0$F/Gas Mark 4.

Heat the oil in a non-stick pan; add the ginger, garlic and onion and sauté till golden.

Add the tomato, chilli powder, two tablespoons water and salt.

Stir and add the eggs and fresh coriander. Cook, stirring, till the eggs are well scrambled. Divide the mixture into four equal portions.

Cut a thin slice off the top of the buns and scoop out the crumbs to form bread cups.

Apply the melted butter on the inside of the cups and spoon one portion of the filling into each like a mound.

Drizzle a tablespoon of white sauce on top of each mound and grill the buns in the preheated oven till the top turns a light golden. Serve hot.

# Mulligatawny Soup

**Iron Content: 10.4 mg**

**ingredients**

500 grams boneless lamb, chopped

½ teaspoon turmeric powder

10 cups lamb white stock

5 teaspoons coriander powder

A pinch of fenugreek seeds

2 teaspoons cumin seeds

1 inch cinnamon stick

Salt to taste

A pinch of black pepper powder

2 inches ginger, chopped

4-5 garlic cloves, chopped

2 medium onions, sliced

2 sprigs curry leaves

4-5 medium tomatoes, chopped

½ cup Coconut Milk (see below)

4 teaspoons ghee

1 teaspoon lemon juice

**method**

Place the lamb in a deep non-stick pan. Add the turmeric powder and the stock and bring it to a boil. Reduce heat and cook till the lamb is tender.

Add the coriander powder, fenugreek seeds, cumin seeds and cinnamon. Divide the salt, pepper, ginger, garlic, onions, curry leaves and tomatoes in two portions and add one portion to the pan.

Let the mixture simmer for fifteen minutes or till the tomatoes soften. Remove from heat and remove the lamb pieces. Pass the liquid through a soup strainer into another deep non-stick pan. Put lamb pieces back into the soup. Add the coconut milk and stir.

Heat the ghee in a non-stick pan and sauté the remaining onions to a golden brown colour and add to the soup along with the lemon juice and the remaining salt, pepper, ginger, garlic, curry leaves and tomatoes. Increase heat and let the soup boil for five minutes.

Serve hot with boiled rice.

**Coconut Milk**

Process 1 cup grated fresh coconut in a blender with ¼ cup warm water. Pass the ground coconut through a piece of muslin or strainer pressing firmly to extract all the juice, or first milk. Add ¼ cup of warm water to the strained coconut to get the second, thinner milk from the same solids.

26

# Beans And Vegetable Soup

**Iron Content: 13.6 mg**

**ingredients**

⅓ cup red kidney beans, soaked

2 medium tomatoes, puréed

1 medium carrot, cut into ¼-inch pieces

10-15 French beans, cut into ¼-inch pieces

½ cup button mushrooms, chopped

1 medium green capsicum, ¼-inch pieces

1 medium cucumber, seeded, ¼-inch pieces

1 medium onion

4 garlic cloves

¼ cup fresh coriander leaves

3 cups Vegetable Stock (page 27) or water

Salt to taste

½ teaspoon red chilli powder

100 grams tofu, cut into ¼-inch pieces

**method**

Pressure-cook the kidney beans with onion and garlic till soft. Drain and reserve the stock. Mash the kidney beans lightly and set aside.

Separate the coriander leaves from the stems. Discard the stems and reserve the leaves for garnishing. Mix lightly mashed kidney beans with the reserved stock. Stir in the puréed tomatoes and bring the mixture to a boil.

Add the carrot, French beans and vegetable stock or water. Continue to simmer till the carrots are cooked. Stir in mushrooms, salt, chilli powder and capsicum.

Simmer for five minutes and add the cucumber and tofu. Serve hot garnished with fresh coriander leaves.

**Vegetable Stock**

Peel, wash and chop 1 onion, ½ medium carrot, 2-3 inch celery stalk and 2-3 garlic cloves. Place in a non-stick pan with 1 bay leaf, 5-6 peppercorns, 2-3 cloves and 5 cups of water and bring to a boil. Lower heat and simmer for 15 minutes and strain. Cool and store in a refrigerator till further use.

# Spinach And Tofu Soup

**Iron Content: 10.3 mg**

**ingredients**

250 grams spinach, shredded roughly

100 grams bean curd (tofu)

½ tablespoon oil

½ inch ginger, finely chopped

2-3 garlic cloves, finely chopped

4-5 cups Vegetable Stock (page 27)

¼ teaspoon MSG (optional)

1 tablespoon soy sauce

½ teaspoon white pepper powder

Salt to taste

**method**

Cut the tofu into one-fourth-inch thick slices and further into one-inch triangles.

Heat the oil in a non-stick wok or a non-stick pan; add the ginger and garlic and stir-fry for half a minute.

Stir in the vegetable stock and bring to a boil. Lower the heat, add the tofu, MSG, soy sauce, white pepper powder and salt and simmer for two to three minutes.

Add the spinach leaves and continue to cook for a minute, stirring gently.

Serve hot.

# Sweet Corn Soup With Mixed Vegetables And Tofu



**Iron Content: 15.7 mg**

**ingredients**

150 grams cream-style sweet corn

½ cup sweet corn kernels

¼ small cabbage, chopped

¼ medium carrot, chopped

100 grams bean curd, cut into ½-inch pieces

2 tablespoons oil

4-5 cups Vegetable Stock (page 27)

Salt to taste

¼ teaspoon white pepper powder

½ tablespoon sugar

¼ teaspoon MSG (optional)

3 tablespoons cornflour

1 stalk spring onion greens, chopped

**method**

Heat the oil in a non-stick wok; add the sweet corn kernels, cabbage and carrot and stir-fry for two minutes. Stir in the vegetable stock and bring to a boil.

Mix in the cream-style corn and continue to cook for two to three minutes.

Add the salt, white pepper powder, sugar and MSG. Add the bean curd and stir in the cornflour, mixed with half a cup of water.

Cook over high heat, stirring continuously, for one minute, or until the soup thickens.

Serve piping hot, garnished with spring onion greens.

# Pepper Rasam

**Iron Content: 3.5 mg**

**ingredients**

10-12 peppercorns, coarsely powdered

3 tablespoons split pigeon peas

1 teaspoon split Bengal gram

1 teaspoon skinless split black gram

6-7 dried red chillies

¼ teaspoon fenugreek seeds

½ teaspoon cumin seeds

¾ teaspoon mustard seeds

1 teaspoon coriander seeds

1 tablespoon oil

3 garlic cloves, crushed

10 curry leaves

Salt to taste

¼ teaspoon turmeric powder

2 tablespoons tamarind pulp

1 tablespoon jaggery, grated

**Seasoning**

1 tablespoon oil

½ teaspoon mustard seeds

2 dried red chillies

¼ teaspoon asafoetida

10 curry leaves

**method**

Soak the pigeon peas in one cup of water for half an hour and pressure-cook in one cup of water. Mash well and set aside.

Dry-roast and powder the split Bengal gram, split black gram, red chillies, fenugreek seeds, cumin seeds, half a teaspoon of mustard seeds and coriander seeds.

Heat the oil in a non-stick *kadai* and add the garlic, remaining mustard seeds, crushed peppercorns and curry leaves.

When the mustard seeds start to splutter, add the mashed *dal*, the *masala* powder mixed with a little water, salt, turmeric powder, tamarind pulp and jaggery. Mix well and stir in five cups of water.

Bring the mixture to a boil, lower the heat and simmer for ten to fifteen minutes. Strain the soup through a piece of muslin.

For the seasoning, heat the oil in a non-stick pan. Add the mustard seeds, and when they start to splutter, add the red chillies, asafoetida and curry leaves. Pour over the *rasum*. Serve hot.

# Tomato Egg Drop Soup

**Iron Content: 28.3 mg**

**ingredients**

4 medium tomatoes, chopped

2 eggs, lightly whisked

2 tablespoons oil

1 inch ginger (optional), peeled and chopped

2-3 garlic cloves, chopped

½ medium onion, chopped

4 tablespoons tomato sauce

4 cups Vegetable Stock (page 27)

Salt to taste

1 teaspoon sugar

¼ teaspoon MSG (optional)

½ teaspoon white pepper powder

2 tablespoons cornflour

2 tablespoons white vinegar

1 tablespoon fresh coriander leaves, chopped

**method**

Heat the oil in a non-stick wok; add the ginger and garlic and stir-fry for one minute. Add the onion and continue to stir-fry for one minute more.

Add the tomatoes and tomato sauce and cook on high heat for two to three minutes. Stir in three and a half cups of vegetable stock and bring to a boil. Add salt to taste, sugar, MSG and white pepper powder.

Mix the cornflour and remaining vegetable stock. Add to the pan and cook for one minute, or until the soup thickens, stirring continuously.

Stir in the vinegar. Pour the whisked egg in a steady stream into the hot soup, stirring gently to form egg threads. The egg will coagulate and float to the top.

Serve hot, garnished with chopped coriander.

# Shrimp And Coriander Soup

**Iron Content: 7 mg**

## ingredients

8 medium shrimps, peeled and halved lengthways

¼ cup fresh coriander, chopped

1 tablespoon cornflour

1 teaspoon oil

1 inch ginger, chopped

2-3 garlic cloves, chopped

1 inch leek, cut into thin strips

1 celery stalk, cut into thin strips

1 green chilli, seeded and cut into thin strips

6 cups fish stock

½ teaspoon white pepper powder

¼ teaspoon MSG (optional)

Salt to taste

1 tablespoon lemon juice

## method

Mix the cornflour in half a cup of water. Set aside.

Heat the oil in a non-stick pan; add the ginger and garlic and stir-fry for one minute.

Add the leek, celery and green chilli and continue to stir-fry for half a minute. Add the fish stock and bring to a boil.

Lower the heat, add the white pepper powder, MSG and salt to taste.

Simmer for four to five minutes, stirring occasionally.

Add the shrimps and cook for a minute, stirring gently. Stir in the cornflour mixture and continue to cook for a minute more. Add the fresh coriander.

Simmer the soup for half a minute and stir in the lemon juice and serve piping hot.

# Four Bean Salad

**Iron Content: 6.5 mg**

## ingredients

¼ cup green gram

¼ cup black-eyed beans

¼ cup red kidney beans

100 grams French beans, cut into ¼-inch pieces

Salt to taste

3 tablespoons lemon juice

½ cup fresh coriander, chopped

¼ cup fresh mint, chopped

2 green chillies, chopped

1½ teaspoons *chaat masala*

1 medium onion, cut into ¼-inch pieces

## method

Soak the beans separately in plenty of water overnight, or for at least six hours. Soak the green gram for about two hours.

Boil separately the three types of soaked beans and French beans in salted water till tender. Drain immediately and refresh in cold water. Drain and set aside to cool.

Dilute the lemon juice with an equal amount of water. Stir in the chopped coriander, mint, green chillies and *chaat masala*. Mix well and refrigerate for at least one hour.

Mix all the cooked beans, onion and dressing. Toss to coat the salad well with the dressing.

Chef's Tip: Do not hesitate to throw away the water in which you cook pulses as it is more harmful than beneficial. However, you may reserve the liquid in which you cooked the French beans to use as stock in another recipe.

# Barley And Crunchy Nut Salad



**Iron Content: 11.7 mg**

**ingredients**

1 cup barley

½ cup peanuts, roasted

Salt to taste

2 large cucumbers, seeded, cut into small pieces

2 large tomatoes, seeded, cut into small pieces

2 inches celery stalk, chopped

2 tablespoons chopped fresh coriander

5-6 black peppercorns, crushed

2 teaspoons lemon juice

4 large lettuce leaves

**method**

Soak the barley in three cups of water for six hours. Drain and pressure-cook with three cups of water and salt till almost done. Drain and set aside to cool.

In a large bowl, combine together the barley, cucumbers, tomatoes, peanuts, celery, chopped coriander, salt, crushed peppercorns and lemon juice and toss well.

Arrange the lettuce leaves on a serving platter, transfer the tossed salad onto the lettuce bed and serve immediately.

# 42 Chicken And Sweet Potato Salad

**Iron Content: 10.3 mg**

## ingredients

2 boneless chicken breasts, boiled

2 large sweet potatoes, boiled

150 grams cottage cheese,
cut into cubes

4 tablespoons mayonnaise

1 teaspoon French mustard

¼ teaspoon white pepper powder

½ teaspoon sugar

Salt to taste

2 spring onion greens, chopped

## method

Cut the chicken into match stick-size strips and set aside.

Peel the boiled sweet potatoes and cut into half-inch cubes and set aside.

Mix the mayonnaise, French mustard, white pepper powder, sugar and salt in a food processor and blend at high speed until smooth. Transfer the mixture into a large bowl.

Add the chicken, sweet potato, cottage cheese and chopped spring onions greens and toss.

Serve chilled.

# Five Sprouts Salad

**Iron Content: 28.3 mg**

## ingredients

¼ cup sprouted brown Bengal gram
¼ cup sprouted white peas
½ cup sprouted green gram
½ cup sprouted red lentil
½ cup sprouted brown gram
Salt to taste
1 medium tomato, finely chopped
1 medium onion, finely chopped
1 tablespoon lemon juice
Black salt to taste
1 teaspoon *chaat masala*
½ teaspoon red chilli powder
½ cup crushed roasted peanuts
2 tablespoons chopped fresh coriander

## method

Boil four cups of water in a deep non-stick pan.

Add the salt, brown Bengal gram and white peas and boil for ten to fifteen minutes.

Add the green gram, red lentil and brown gram and continue to boil for seven to eight minutes more.

Drain and transfer into a large bowl.

Add the tomato, onion, lemon juice, black salt, *chaat masala*, chilli powder and peanuts and mix.

Serve garnished with chopped coriander.

# Chicken Spinach Salad

**Iron Content: 13.1 mg**

**ingredients**

2 boneless skinless chicken breasts

8-10 fresh baby spinach leaves, hand torn

5 tablespoon oil

Salt to taste

¼ teaspoon crushed black peppercorns

1 sprig fresh rosemary, finely chopped

3-4 fresh basil leaves, finely chopped

2 sprigs fresh thyme, finely chopped

4 teaspoons olive oil

2 teaspoons lemon juice

Salt to taste

¼ teaspoon white pepper powder

¼ teaspoon sugar

5-6 green olives

5-6 black olives

5-6 stuffed olives

100 grams lettuce leaves, hand torn

**method**

Pat the chicken dry with an absorbent kitchen towel.

Marinate the chicken in a mixture of one teaspoon of oil, salt, crushed peppercorns and half teaspoon each of the chopped fresh rosemary, basil and thyme. Place in the refrigerator for an hour.

To prepare the dressing, mix together four teaspoons of olive oil, lemon juice, salt, white pepper powder, sugar and the remaining fresh herbs.

Pre-heat the grill or non-stick *tawa* on medium heat. Cook the chicken breasts for five to seven minutes or until done, turning once or twice, taking care that it remains juicy.

Take them off the heat, allow to cool and then cut into one-inch pieces. Place them in a bowl.

Add the olives, lettuce, spinach leaves and the dressing. Toss lightly and serve immediately.

# Hara Bhara Kabab

**Iron Content: 5.2 mg**

## ingredients

¾ cup shelled green peas, boiled and mashed

1 cup blanched and chopped fresh spinach leaves

3 medium potatoes, boiled, peeled and grated

2 green chillies, chopped

2 tablespoons chopped fresh coriander

1 inch ginger, chopped

1 teaspoon *chaat masala*

Salt to taste

2 tablespoons cornflour

2 tablespoons oil

## method

Place the peas, spinach and potatoes in a deep bowl and mix well.

Add the chillies, chopped coriander, ginger, *chaat masala* and salt. Mix well. Add the cornflour and mix into a smooth soft dough.

Divide the spinach mixture into twelve equal portions. Shape each portion into a ball and then press it between your palms to give it a flat round shape that looks like a thick disc.

Heat one teaspoon of oil in a non-stick pan. Place six kababs on the pan, keeping a little distance between each.

Drizzle one more teaspoon of oil all around the kababs and cook for two to three minutes or till the underside is golden brown.

Then, turn each over and drizzle more oil all around and cook till the other side becomes golden brown. Drain on absorbent paper. Similarly cook the remaining kababs.

Serve immediately.

# Green Chana Chaat

**Iron Content: 13.5 mg**

**ingredients**

1½ cups green Bengal gram, soaked overnight

2 medium onions, chopped

2 medium tomatoes, chopped

2-3 green chillies, chopped

2 tablespoons chopped fresh coriander

Black salt to taste

1 teaspoon roasted cumin powder

1 teaspoon *chaat masala*

½ teaspoon red chilli powder

2 tablespoons lemon juice

**method**

Pressure-cook the soaked green Bengal gram in three cups of water till the pressure is released two to three times (two to three whistles) or till done.

Transfer to a non-stick *kadai* and simmer till all the water evaporates.

Transfer the hot *chana* to a bowl. Add the onions, tomatoes, green chillies, chopped coriander, black salt, roasted cumin powder, *chaat masala*, chilli powder and lemon juice and mix well. Serve immediately.

Chef's Tip: When in season, use the fresh green Bengal gram to make this *chaat*.

# Jacket Potatoes With Baked Beans Stuffing



**Iron Content: 11.3 mg**

## ingredients

4 large potatoes

1 cup baked beans

1 bay leaf

1 medium onion, chopped

6 garlic cloves, chopped

1 tablespoon tomato ketchup

1 teaspoon sea salt

¼ teaspoon black pepper powder

## method

Parboil the potatoes with skin. Drain, cool and halve. Scoop out the centre leaving a thick wall around.

Pre-heat the oven to 200°C/400°F/Gas Mark 6.

Heat a non-stick pan; add the bay leaf, onion and garlic and cook till the onion turns a light brown.

Add the tomato ketchup and mix well.

Add the baked beans, sea salt, pepper powder and stir. Bring it to a boil.

Cool slightly. Fill the stuffing into the scooped out potato halves.

Arrange them on a baking tray and bake in the preheated oven for fifteen to twenty minutes. Serve hot.

# Tacos With Refried Beans, Salsa And Crispy Vegetables

**Iron Content: 26.1 mg**

## ingredients

8 tacos shells

2 cups soaked red kidney beans

4 garlic cloves

1 bay leaf

3 tablespoons oil

3 medium onions, chopped

Salt to taste

10-12 black peppercorns, freshly ground

½ small iceberg lettuce, shredded

1 medium carrot, grated

½ small red cabbage, shredded

¼ cup salsa

½ cup grated Cheddar cheese

## method

Place the kidney beans in a large non-stick pan with garlic and bay leaf. Cover with cold water and bring to a boil. Simmer and cook gently until the beans are very tender.

Drain the beans, reserving the liquid. Discard the bay leaf.

Mash the beans coarsely with a potato masher or process in a blender, adding some of the reserved liquid.

Heat oil in another non-stick pan. Add the onions and sauté till translucent.

Add the beans and the seasoning and mix well. Simmer for a few minutes. Take the pan off the heat. Keep warm.

Mix together the iceberg lettuce, carrot and red cabbage. Chill in a refrigerator.

Take the taco shells; spoon the prepared refried beans evenly into the shells.

Top it up with salsa and then sprinkle cheese. Finally top it up with crispy vegetables and serve immediately.

# Pashtuni Chana Tikki

**Iron Content: 16.7 mg**

## ingredients

1¼ cups chickpeas, soaked overnight

2 teaspoons tea leaves

12 pieces dried Indian gooseberries

3 green cardamoms

1 black cardamom

2 bay leaves

1 inch cinnamon

1 medium potato, boiled, peeled and mashed

1 tablespoon coriander powder

2 teaspoons Kashmiri red chilli powder

Salt to taste

1 tablespoon lemon juice

4 tablespoons chopped fresh coriander

4 green chillies, finely chopped

1½ inch ginger piece, chopped

1 teaspoon *chhole masala*

1 teaspoon *chaat masala*

1 teaspoon dried mango powder

12 cashew nuts, chopped

2 tablespoons raisins, chopped

Oil for shallow-frying

Mint chutney, as required

1 large onion, finely sliced

**method**

Drain the chickpeas and transfer to a pressure cooker. Tie up the tea leaves, gooseberries, cardamoms, bay leaves and cinnamon in a piece of muslin to make a *potli* and add along with five cups of water. Cover the cooker with the lid and cook under pressure, on low heat, till pressure is released eight to ten times (8-10 whistles).

Open the lid when the pressure reduces completely, discard the spice *potli*, strain the chickpeas. Use the stock for some other dish.

Mince the boiled chickpeas in a mincer. Transfer into a bowl and add the potato, coriander powder, chilli powder, salt, lemon juice, two tablespoons chopped coriander and mix well. Add the green chillies and ginger and mix well. Add the *chhole masala, chaat masala* and dried mango powder and mix well.

For the stuffing, mix together the cashew nuts, raisins and the remaining chopped coriander well. Divide both the chickpea mixture and the stuffing into twelve portions each. Stuff each chickpea portion with a portion of the stuffing and shape into a *tikki*.

Heat a little oil in a non-stick pan and place the *tikki*, four at a time, on it and shallow-fry, turning sides a few times, till both sides are golden. Drain on absorbent paper. Serve hot with mint chutney and onion slices.

# Palak Pakore Ki Chaat

**Iron Content: 18.9 mg**

**ingredients**

16-20 fresh medium spinach leaves

1½ cups coarsely ground gram flour

Salt to taste

½ teaspoon red chilli powder

¼ teaspoon turmeric powder

½ teaspoon carom seeds

A pinch of asafoetida

Oil for deep-frying

1 cup yogurt

2 teaspoons roasted cumin seed powder

4 tablespoons green chutney

4 tablespoons date and tamarind chutney

3 medium onions, chopped

½ cup *sev*

½ cup fresh coriander leaves, chopped

**method**

Place the gram flour in a bowl with the salt, chilli powder, turmeric powder, carom seeds and asafoetida. Add enough water to make a thin batter.

Heat sufficient oil in a non-stick *kadai*. Coat both the sides of each spinach leaf with the batter and deep-fry in hot oil till golden brown and crisp. Drain on absorbent paper.

Whisk the yogurt with salt to taste.

To serve, place two *palak pakore* on each serving plate.

Cover with two to three tablespoons of whisked yogurt and sprinkle with roasted cumin seed powder.

Top with dollops of green chutney and date and tamarind chutney.

Sprinkle a little chopped onion and cover liberally with *sev*. Garnish with chopped coriander and serve immediately.

# Spinach Omelette

**Iron Content: 13.2 mg**

## ingredients

### Omelette

4 eggs
Salt to taste
1 tablespoon flour
1 cup milk

### Spinach Filling

2 tablespoons spinach (can use left over *palak paneer* for instance)
1 small tomato, chopped
1 tablespoon cheddar cheese
1 tablespoon butter
1 tablespoon refined flour
½ cup milk
¼ teaspoon salt
½ teaspoon pepper, crushed
1 tablespoon grated cheddar cheese

## method

Beat the eggs thoroughly with salt and flour. Stir in the milk gradually.

Pour the mixture in a greased oven-proof dish and bake in a moderate oven at 130⁰C/250⁰F/ Gas Mark ½ for about forty-five minutes till top is browned.

For the spinach filling, cook the spinach, tomato and cheddar cheese in a non-stick pan till tender. Drain; set aside and reserve the liquid.

Heat the butter in non-stick pan, add the refined flour and gradually stir in the milk and liquid from the spinach. Season and stir continuously till the sauce thickens.

Add spinach-tomato-cheese mixture to the white sauce and pour over the omelette. Top with grated cheese, grill for a minute and serve immediately.

# Palak Methi Puri



**Iron Content: 13.2 mg**

## ingredients

½ cup fresh spinach purée

½ cup chopped fresh fenugreek leaves

1½ cups whole-wheat flour

1 teaspoon ginger-green chilli paste

Salt to taste

1 tablespoon oil + for deep-frying

## method

Combine together the flour, spinach purée, fenugreek leaves, ginger-green chilli paste, salt and one tablespoon of oil and knead into a firm dough.

Cover with a damp cloth and rest the dough for about ten minutes. Divide into sixteen equal portions and shape into balls. Roll out each into four-inch round *puri*.

Heat sufficient oil in a non-stick *kadai* and deep-fry the *puri*, one by one, on medium heat. Drain on absorbent paper.

Serve hot.

# Chettinaad Kozhi Varuval

**Iron Content: 12.5 mg**

## ingredients

1 whole (800 grams) chicken

2 medium onions, roughly chopped

1 inch ginger, roughly chopped

4-6 garlic cloves, roughly chopped

4 green chillies, roughly chopped

4-6 dried red chillies

½ teaspoon turmeric powder

1 tablespoon lemon juice

2 tablespoons rice flour

Salt to taste

10-12 curry leaves, finely shredded

Oil for shallow-frying

## method

Split the chicken through the backbone and the breast, into two equal halves.

Make three or four half-inch deep cuts on the breast and leg pieces.

Grind the onions, ginger, garlic, green chillies and red chillies with a little water to a smooth paste.

Mix the turmeric powder, lemon juice, rice flour and salt into the *masala* paste.

Coat the chicken liberally with the paste and leave to marinate for two or three hours, preferably in a refrigerator.

Mix the shredded curry leaves into the chicken.

Heat the oil in a non-stick *kadai*; add the marinated chicken and sauté over high heat for two minutes on both sides to seal the juices.

Lower heat to medium, cover with a lid and cook for fifteen to twenty minutes, turning over and basting frequently with the remaining marinade. Sprinkle a little water if the chicken starts drying out.

Cook over high heat for the last few minutes, so that the surface of the chicken is crisp and golden brown.

Cut into smaller pieces and serve hot.

# Mini Falafel Burgers

**Iron Content: 37.6 mg**

**ingredients**

1 cup chickpeas, soaked overnight

2-3 garlic cloves, chopped

2 tablespoons chopped fresh coriander

2 tablespoons chopped fresh parsley

4-5 stalks spring onion greens, chopped

¼ cup breadcrumbs

A small pinch of soda bicarbonate

½ teaspoon roasted cumin powder

Salt to taste

¼ teaspoon black pepper powder

½ teaspoon paprika

Oil for deep-frying

**Yogurt sauce**

½ cup drained (hung) yogurt

2 tablespoons cream

1 tablespoon chopped fresh coriander

3-4 garlic cloves, chopped

1 teaspoon chopped fresh parsley

Salt to taste

½ tablespoon lemon juice

**To serve**

1 medium unpeeled cucumber, sliced into ribbons

8 mini burger buns

Butter, as required

4 lettuce leaves, halved

2 cheese slices, quartered

1 medium cucumber, sliced

1 large tomato, sliced

**method**

Drain the chickpeas and spread on a kitchen towel to dry.

Process the chickpeas along with garlic, coriander, parsley, spring onion greens and breadcrumbs in a food processor to a coarse mixture.

Add the soda bicarbonate and cumin powder and mix well. Season with salt, pepper and paprika. Knead the mixture well and place in a refrigerator to chill for a couple of hours.

Shape tablespoonfuls of the chilled mixture into round patties with the help of two tablespoons moistened with water. Arrange on a greased plate and place in a refrigerator till ready to fry.

Heat plenty of oil in a non-stick *kadai* and deep-fry the falafels till golden brown. Drain on absorbent paper. Mix together all the ingredients for the yogurt sauce and chill till required. Apply salt to the cucumber ribbons and set aside. Cut the burger buns into half and spread the cut sides with butter.

On the bottom half of each bun place a lettuce leaf, a quartered cheese slice, cucumber slice and tomato slice.

Place a fried falafel on the vegetable slices and top with yogurt sauce and cucumber ribbons. Cover with the top half of the bun.

Serve immediately.

Chef's Tip: In place of mini burgers you can also use small round buns.

# Chicken Burger



**Iron Content: 14 mg**

**ingredients**

1½ cups minced chicken

1 small onion, finely chopped

1 garlic clove, finely chopped

1 small apple, peeled and grated

¼ cup cooked rice

Salt to taste

A pinch of dried basil

A pinch of dried oregano

½ teaspoon black pepper powder

Oil for shallow-frying

**Sauce**

1 tablespoon oil

1 inch ginger, grated

1 cup orange juice

1 tablespoon brown sugar

Salt to taste

1 teaspoon dark soy sauce

¼ cup tomato purée

½ teaspoon red chilli powder

1 tablespoon cornflour

**To serve**

4 buns

4 lettuce leaves

**method**

Place the minced chicken, onion, garlic, apple, boiled rice in a bowl and mix thoroughly. Add the salt, basil, oregano, pepper powder and mix well.

Divide the mixture into four equal portions and shape into patties. Heat sufficient oil in a non-stick pan and shallow-fry the patties on both sides till golden brown on both sides. Drain on absorbent paper.

To make the sauce, heat the oil in another non-stick pan and add the ginger. Add the orange juice, brown sugar, salt, soy sauce and mix well. Add the tomato purée, chilli powder and mix. Simmer till it is slightly reduced in quantity. Add the cornflour mixed in a little water and mix till the sauce is sufficiently thick.

Slit the buns into two. Place a lettuce leaf over one half. Place the chicken burger over it and cover with the other half. Serve immediately with the sauce. (Place sliced cucumber and sliced tomatoes etc. as required (optional)).

# Multigrain Footlong With Herbed Chicken

**Iron Content: 15.8 mg**

**ingredients**

2 multigrain footlong rolls

1½ teaspoons dried mixed herbs

2 cups boiled and shredded chicken

2 tablespoons olive oil

40-45 garlic cloves, finely chopped

1½ teaspoons red chilli flakes

Salt to taste

2 teaspoons crushed black peppercorns

8 tablespoons mayonnaise

16 lettuce leaves, shredded

4 cheese slices

Tomato ketchup, as required

Mustard sauce, as required

**method**

Heat the olive oil in a non-stick pan. Add the garlic and sauté till light brown.

Add the red chilli flakes, dried herbs, salt, crushed peppercorns and shredded chicken and sauté for a minute and remove from heat.

Slit the footlong bread lengthways without cutting through.

Apply the mayonnaise on both the inner sides. Cover the base with the lettuce. Place cheese slices over the lettuce and top it up with the chicken mixture.

Drizzle tomato ketchup and mustard sauce over it and press the top over gently. Cut each footlong into half and serve immediately.

# Palak Aur Gajar Pulao

**Iron Content: 10.6 mg**

**ingredients**

700 grams fresh spinach leaves, chopped

4 medium carrots, cut into ½-inch cubes

1½ cups rice, soaked

2 tablespoons oil

Salt to taste

**Masala**

3 cloves

1 inch cinnamon

1 teaspoon coriander seeds

1 teaspoon cumin seeds

1 bay leaf

1 large onion, chopped

1 inch ginger, chopped

10 garlic cloves

2 green chillies, chopped

**method**

For the *masala*, dry-roast the cloves, cinnamon, coriander seeds, cumin seeds and bay leaf for three or four minutes.

Grind the roasted spices together with the onion, ginger, garlic, green chillies and one-fourth cup of water to a smooth paste.

Heat the oil in a deep non-stick pan and sauté the *masala* paste till the oil separates. Add the carrots and sauté for a couple of minutes.

Add the soaked rice, salt to taste and three cups of water and stir well. Cover and cook for five minutes. Stir in the spinach leaves.

Cover and cook until all the water has been absorbed. Serve hot.

# Corn Capsicum Masala

**Iron Content: 15.2 mg**

## ingredients

300 grams corn kernels

2 medium green capsicums, cut into ½-inch pieces

3 tablespoons oil

½ teaspoon cumin seeds

3 medium onions, chopped

2 tablespoons ginger paste

1 tablespoon garlic paste

1 teaspoon red chilli powder

1 tablespoon coriander powder

1 teaspoon cumin powder

½ teaspoon turmeric powder

2 medium tomatoes, puréed

½ cup *khoya/mawa*

1 teaspoon *garam masala* powder

Salt to taste

¼ cup fresh cream

¼ cup fresh coriander leaves, chopped

## method

Boil the corn kernels in three cups of water till tender. Drain and set aside.

Heat the oil in a non-stick *kadai*; add the cumin seeds. When cumin seeds begin to change colour, add the onions and sauté till golden brown.

Add the ginger and garlic pastes and cook for two to three minutes. Add the chilli powder, coriander powder, cumin powder and turmeric powder. Stir-fry for a few seconds. Add the tomato purée and cook, stirring continuously, till the oil separates. Add the *mawa* and half cup of water, mix well and cook for a minute.

Add the capsicum and mix well. Finally add the boiled corn, *garam masala* powder and salt. Mix and cook on low heat for four to five minutes.

Stir in the fresh cream and chopped coriander. Serve hot.

Chef's Tip: This recipe is high on calories. Reduce the calories by using milk instead of the *mawa* and cream.

# Paneer Kofta In Spinach Curry

**Iron Content: 15.5 mg**

**ingredients**

200 grams cottage cheese

500 grams spinach

2 green chillies, roughly chopped

2 medium potatoes, boiled, peeled and mashed

3 tablespoons cornflour

½ teaspoon red chilli powder

½ inch ginger, finely chopped

Salt to taste

½ teaspoon white pepper powder

12-15 cashew nuts, roughly chopped

12-15 raisins, roughly chopped

3 tablespoons oil + for deep-frying

½ teaspoon caraway seeds

5-6 garlic cloves, finely chopped

½ cup tomato purée

½ teaspoon turmeric powder

1 teaspoon coriander powder

1 teaspoon *garam masala* powder

¼ cup fresh cream

**method**

Mash the cottage cheese thoroughly or pass through a sieve.

Blanch the spinach in sufficient water, refresh under running water and drain well. Grind to a smooth purée along with green chillies.

Mix together the cottage cheese and potatoes along with cornflour, chilli powder, ginger, salt and white pepper powder. Divide the mixture into sixteen even-sized balls. Stuff each ball with cashew nuts and raisins.

Heat sufficient oil in a non-stick *kadai* and deep-fry the balls a few at a time until golden brown. Drain on an absorbent paper and set aside. Heat three tablespoons of oil in a non-stick *handi*; add the caraway seeds and garlic and stir-fry. Add spinach purée and cook for about two to three minutes. Stir in the tomato purée and mix well.

Add the turmeric powder, coriander powder and salt. Cook for four to five minutes. Add one cup of water and bring to a boil. Reduce heat and allow to simmer for five to seven minutes.

Stir in the *garam masala* powder and cook till curry is reduced to half. Reduce heat, stir in the cream and cook for half a minute. Remove from heat.

Arrange the *kofte* in a serving dish. Pour hot gravy on top and serve hot.

# Palak Chole

**Iron Content: 14.4 mg**

**ingredients**

500 grams spinach

1 cup chickpeas, soaked

3-4 green chillies

1 inch ginger

4-5 garlic cloves

2 tablespoons ghee

1 teaspoon cumin seeds

1 cup tomato purée

1 teaspoon red chilli powder

1 teaspoon *garam masala* powder

Salt to taste

**method**

Drain the chickpeas; add three cups of water and pressure-cook till done. Drain and refresh. Set aside.

Blanch the spinach in boiling water for two minutes. Drain, refresh and blend to a purée. Grind the green chillies, ginger and garlic to a coarse paste using a little water.

Heat the ghee in a non-stick *kadai*; add the cumin seeds and sauté till it changes colour.

Add the green chilli-ginger-garlic paste and fry for a minute. Add tomato purée, chilli powder, *garam masala* powder and salt and fry for a few minutes or till the ghee separates from the *masala*.

Add the spinach purée and chickpeas and stir gently. Cover and allow simmering on low heat for five to six minutes. Serve hot.

# Pesto Vegetable Pasta



**Iron Content: 14.1 mg**

**ingredients**

200 grams fresh fettucine

3 tablespoon oil

Salt to taste

6 shallots, quartered

1 red capsicum, cut into 1-inch pieces

½ cup corn kernels, boiled

6-8 French beans, cut into ½-inch pieces, boiled

5-6 black peppercorns, freshly crushed

½ cup milk

Parmesan cheese, for garnishing

3-4 fresh basil leaves

**Pesto Sauce**

30-40 (¾ cup) basil leaves

3-4 garlic cloves

Salt to taste

3 tablespoons pine nuts

6 tablespoons olive oil

4-5 black peppercorns

¼ cup Parmesan cheese

**method**

To make the pesto sauce, grind together the fresh basil leaves, garlic and salt.

Add pine nuts, olive oil, peppercorns and Parmesan cheese, one after the other, and grind till all the ingredients are well mixed. Transfer to a bowl. Boil plenty of water in a deep non-stick pan. Add one tablespoon oil, salt and fettucine. Cook till *al dente* (cooked but still firm to the bite).

Heat the remaining olive oil in another non-stick pan; add the shallots and saute for two minutes. Add the capsicum and toss for one minute. Add the pesto sauce and sauté for four to five minutes.

Drain the pasta and add to the pesto.  Toss well so that the sauce coats the pasta. Add corn kernels and French beans. Toss to mix.

Stir in salt and peppercorns. Add the milk and Parmesan cheese. Mix well. Tear the basil leaves and add to the pasta. Toss once again. Serve immediately.

# Masaledaar Aloo, Paneer And Broccoli

**Iron Content: 14.6 mg**

## ingredients

2 medium potatoes, parboiled, peeled and cut into cubes

200 grams cottage cheese, cut into triangles

150 grams broccoli, separated into small florets

2 tablespoons oil

1 teaspoon ginger-garlic paste

10-12 spring onion bulbs, halved and layers separated

Salt to taste

6-8 cherry tomatoes

½ teaspoon red chilli flakes

½ teaspoon black pepper powder

½ teaspoon dried oregano

## method

Heat the oil in a non-stick pan. Add the ginger-garlic paste and spring onions and sauté for a few minutes.

Add the potatoes and salt and sauté for four to five more minutes. Add the broccoli and cook till the potatoes are done.

Add the cottage cheese, cherry tomatoes, red chilli flakes, pepper powder, dried oregano and mix well. Cook for three to four minutes. Add three tablespoons of water and mix. Serve hot.

# Kale Masoor Chawli Ke Patton Ke Saath

**Iron Content: 15.4 mg**

## ingredients

¼ cup whole black lentils, soaked

2 small bunches fresh *chawli* leaves, chopped

¼ teaspoon turmeric powder

Salt to taste

3 teaspoons oil

1 teaspoon cumin seeds

½ cup Coconut Milk (page 25)

½ teaspoon lemon juice

### Paste

1 tablespoon coriander seeds

½ tablespoon cumin seeds

6-8 garlic cloves

½ inch ginger

3 dried Kashmiri red chillies, broken

## method

For the paste, place the coriander seeds, cumin seeds, garlic cloves, ginger, dried red chillies in a blender jar and grind to a smooth paste. Add water only if required.

Add the turmeric powder, salt and half cup water to the lentils and pressure-cook till pressure is released thrice (three whistles). Allow to cool.

Heat the oil in a non-stick pan and add the cumin seeds. When the seeds begin to change colour, add the *chawli* leaves and cook for ten minutes, stirring continuously.

Add the cooked lentils to the pan. Stir and add the prepared paste and cook for five to seven more minutes, stirring continuously.

Add the coconut milk and salt and simmer for two to three minutes. Take the pan off the heat, add the lemon juice and mix well. Serve hot.

# Tofu Chana Dal

**Iron Content: 20.9 mg**

**ingredients**

200 grams bean curd (tofu), cut into small cubes

¾ cup split Bengal gram

1 teaspoon oil

½ teaspoon mustard seeds

10–12 curry leaves

2 pinches of asafoetida

½ level teaspoon salt

¼ teaspoon turmeric powder

1 tablespoon lemon juice

¼ cup hand torn fresh mint leaves

**method**

Soak the split Bengal gram in two cups of water for three to four hours.

Heat one teaspoon oil in a non-stick pan and add the mustard seeds and curry leaves. As the seeds begin to splutter, stir in the asafoetida. Add the drained Bengal gram and salt and sauté for two minutes.

Stir in the turmeric powder and add half cup of water. Cover, and cook for ten to twelve minutes, or until the Bengal gram is done.

Add the tofu, lemon juice and mint leaves. Cook for half a minute, remove from heat and serve.

# Masoor Keema Pulao



**Iron Content: 15.2 mg**

**ingredients**

$^{1}/_{3}$ cup whole lentils, soaked overnight and boiled

225 grams minced mutton

1 cup Basmati rice, soaked

1½ tablespoons olive oil/rice bran oil

1½ teaspoons cumin seeds

1½ large onions, chopped

1 teaspoon ginger paste

1 teaspoon garlic paste

1½ large tomatoes, chopped

Salt to taste

1½ teaspoons red chilli powder

1½ teaspoons coriander powder

¼ teaspoon turmeric powder

⅓ cup skimmed milk yogurt, whisked

¾ teaspoon *garam masala* powder

1½ tablespoons chopped fresh coriander

1 tablespoon ghee

3 cloves

3 black peppercorns

1 inch cinnamon

**method**

Drain and boil the rice with four cups of water till almost done. Drain and set aside.

Heat the oil in a non-stick deep pan; add three-fourth teaspoon cumin seeds. When they begin to change colour, add the onions and sauté till golden. Add the ginger paste, garlic paste and sauté for one minute.

Add the tomatoes, salt and sauté till the tomatoes turn pulpy. Add the chilli powder, coriander powder and turmeric powder and sauté for a few seconds. Add the minced mutton and sauté for two minutes. Add the yogurt and cook for three or four minutes. Add half a cup of water, cover and cook till the mutton is tender.

Stir in the *garam masala* powder and whole lentils. Add the chopped coriander and mix well. Spread the rice over the lentils. In a separate pan, heat the ghee. Add the remaining cumin seeds, cloves, peppercorns and cinnamon. Sauté for one minute and pour over the rice.

Cover the pan with aluminium foil and place a lid on it. Place the pan over a hot *tawa* and cook over low heat for ten minutes. Serve hot with *raita*.

# Chicken Cafreal

**Iron Content: 11.8 mg**

**ingredients**

1 (1 kg) chicken, cut into 8 pieces

3 tablespoons oil + for deep-frying

2 medium onions, finely sliced

1 tablespoon coriander seeds

1 teaspoon cumin seeds

6 cloves

8 green cardamoms

8 black peppercorns

1 inch cinnamon

1 inch ginger, roughly chopped

4-5 garlic cloves, roughly chopped

6 green chillies, roughly chopped

Salt to taste

3 tablespoons vinegar

**method**

Make deep incisions on the chicken pieces using a sharp knife.

Heat sufficient oil in a non-stick *kadai* and deep-fry the onions till crisp and golden brown.

Drain onto an absorbent paper and reserve for garnishing.

Dry-roast the coriander seeds, cumin seeds, cloves, cardamoms, peppercorns and cinnamon. Grind with the ginger, garlic and green chillies to a fine paste using a little water.

Add salt to the paste and rub the paste over the chicken and marinate for two to three hours, in a refrigerator. Heat three tablespoons of oil in a non-stick pan; add the marinated chicken and cook, covered, on medium heat stirring occasionally. Add a little warm water if required to prevent scorching. Cook for eight to ten minutes.

When almost done add the vinegar and cook for two to three minutes. Serve hot garnished with the fried onions.

Chef's Tip: You can add a little fresh coriander to the paste for a different taste. I know of a Goan restaurant, which does it and it tastes delicious.

# Kadai Murgh Methi Palak



**Iron Content: 18.7 mg**

**ingredients**

**Chicken tikka**

400 grams boneless chicken, cut into sixteen 1½-inch pieces

2 teaspoons garlic paste

1 teaspoon ginger paste

2 tablespoons Kashmiri red chilli paste

Salt to taste

½ tablespoon lemon juice

½ cup drained (hung) yogurt

1 teaspoon *garam masala* powder

1 tablespoon oil

1 teaspoon turmeric powder

1 teaspoon Kashmiri red chilli powder

1 tablespoon gram flour

Melted butter for basting

**Gravy**

2 medium onions

500 grams fresh spinach leaves, blanched

¼ cup oil

25 garlic cloves, chopped

1⅓ tablespoons Kadai Masala (page 93)

Salt to taste

½ cup fresh tomato purée

200 grams fresh fenugreek leaves, blanched and chopped

½ teaspoon turmeric powder

2 teaspoons Kashmiri red chilli powder

2 teaspoons coriander powder

3 tablespoons butter

1 teaspoon crushed black peppercorns

2 teaspoons *chaat masala*

2 teaspoons dried fenugreek leaves

2 tablespoons cashew nut paste

¼ cup yogurt

1 medium green capsicum, cut into 1-inch pieces

1 medium tomato, cut into 1-inch pieces

¼ cup fresh cream

2 tablespoons chopped fresh coriander

1 teaspoon lemon juice

1 teaspoon red chilli flakes

**method**

To make the chicken *tikka*, preheat oven to 200°C/400°F/Gas Mark 6.

Mix together the garlic paste, ginger paste, red chilli paste, salt, lemon juice, drained yogurt and *garam masala* powder and apply to the chicken pieces. Heat the oil in a small non-stick pan and take it off the heat.

Add the turmeric powder, chilli powder and gram flour and mix well. Add to the chicken and marinate for one hour. Place the chicken pieces on a baking tray and cook in the preheated oven for ten minutes. Baste with melted butter and cook for five minutes more. Set aside.

For the gravy, finely chop one onion and chop the other into one-inch square pieces. Chop two-third of the blanched spinach leaves and make a purée of the remaining spinach leaves. Heat the oil in a non-stick *kadai*; add the garlic and sauté till light brown. Add one tablespoon of *kadai masala*, finely chopped onion and salt and sauté till lightly browned. Add the tomato purée and sauté till the oil separates.

Add the fenugreek leaves and chopped spinach leaves and sauté for two minutes more. Add the turmeric powder, chilli powder, coriander powder and butter and sauté for five minutes. Add the crushed peppercorns, *chaat masala*, dried fenugreek leaves, cashew nut paste, yogurt, spinach purée, onion pieces, capsicum and tomato and mix well.

Add the chicken *tikka* and cream and cook for two to three minutes. Transfer to a serving dish; sprinkle the chopped coriander, remaining *kadai masala*, lemon juice and red chilli flakes and serve hot.

**Kadai Masala**

Dry-roast 2 teaspoons cumin seeds, 2 teaspoons coriander seeds, 8 black peppercorns and 5 dried red chillies. Cool and pound to a coarse powder.

# Goan Chicken Curry

**Iron Content: 14.3 mg**

## ingredients

750 grams chicken on the bone, skinned and cut into 1-inch pieces

1 tablespoon lemon juice

Salt to taste

½ teaspoon black pepper powder

½ cup freshly grated coconut

10 dried red chillies, halved

1 teaspoon cumin seeds

1 tablespoon coriander seeds

¼ teaspoon turmeric powder

2 tablespoons tamarind pulp

1 inch ginger

5-6 garlic cloves

4 tablespoons oil

1 medium onion, finely chopped

2 medium tomatoes, finely chopped

1 cup Coconut Milk (page 25)

## method

Marinate the chicken with lemon juice, salt and pepper powder in a bowl for ten to fifteen minutes.

Grind the coconut, red chillies, cumin seeds, coriander seeds, turmeric powder, tamarind pulp, ginger and garlic to a fine paste with two-third cup of water.

Heat the oil in a non-stick pan. Add the onion and sauté till golden brown.

Add the tomatoes and cook till they are soft. Add the ground *masala* and sauté till the oil separates. Add the chicken and cook on high heat for four to five minutes.

Add three cups of water and salt and mix. Cover and cook till the chicken is almost cooked. Add the coconut milk and cook till the chicken is completely done.

Serve hot with steamed rice.

# Glossary

| English | Hindi |
|---|---|
| Asafoetida | Hing |
| Barley | Jau |
| Bay leaf | Tez patta |
| Beans, black-eyed | Chawli |
| Caraway seeds | Shahi jeera |
| Carom seeds | Ajwain |
| Celery | Ajmud |
| Chickpeas | Kabuli chana |
| Cinnamon | Dalchini |
| Cloves | Laung |
| Coriander seeds | Sabut dhania |
| Dried mango powder | Amchur |
| Fenugreek leaves | Methi bhaji |
| Fenugreek leaves, dried | Kasoori methi |
| Fenugreek seeds | Methi dana |
| Fig | Anjeer |
| Gram flour | Besan |
| Gram, Bengal brown | Desi chane |
| Gram, Bengal green | Hare chane |
| Gram, Bengal split | Chana dal |
| Gram, black split skinless | Dhuli urad dal |
| Gram, brown | Moth/matki |
| Gram, green | Sabut moong dal |
| Indian gooseberries | Amla |
| Leek | Vilayati pyaaz |
| Lentils, red | Masoor dal |
| Lentils, whole | Sabut masoor |
| Mushroom | Khumb/ dhingri |
| Mustard | Sarson/rai |
| Olives | Jaitun |
| Pears | Nashpati |
| Peppercorn, black | Kali mirch |
| Pigeon peas, split | Tuvar/arhar dal |
| Pine nuts | Chilgoza |
| Plums | Aloo bukhare |
| Prunes | Sukhe aloo bukhare |
| Raisins | Kishmish |
| Red kidney beans | Rajma |
| Shrimps | Jhinga |
| Spring onion bulbs | Hare pyaaz |
| Spring onion greens | Hare pyaaz ke patte |
| Sweet corn kernels | Makai ke daane |
| Sweet potato | Shakkar kand |
| Tamarind | Imli |
| Vinegar | Sirka |
| Wheat, broken | Dalia |
| Yogurt | Dahi |